the Invisible Journey

the Invisible Journey
A MEMOIR

ASHLEY DEARKLAND-HESTER

THE INVISIBLE JOURNEY
Published by Purposely Created Publishing Group™

Copyright © 2014 Ashley DeArkland-Hester

ALL RIGHTS RESERVED.

No part of this book may be reproduced, distributed or transmitted in any form by any means, graphics, electronics, or mechanical, including photocopy, recording, taping, or by any information storage or retrieval system, without permission in writing from the publisher, except in the case of reprints in the context of reviews, quotes, or references.

Printed in the United States of America

ISBN (ebook): 978-1-942838-51-7
ISBN (paperback): 978-1-942838-52-4

Special discounts are available on bulk quantity purchases by book clubs, associations and special interest groups.
For details email: sales@publishyourgift.com
or call (888) 949-6228.

For information logon to:
www.PublishYourGift.com

Dedication

In Loving Memory of My Dad, John DeArkland

Table of Contents

Dedication		v
Acknowledgements		ix
Introduction		1
The Kiss of the Devil		5
Chapter 1	Walk With Me	7
Chapter 2	Everyday is a Battle	13
He's Watching Me		18
Chapter 3	Exposing My Reality	19
Set Up		26
Chapter 4	Confrontation	27
Chapter 5	Scattered Thoughts	31
Chapter 6	Discovery & Confirmation	37
Chapter 7	My Intuition is Key	43
Dive Deep		48
Chapter 8	Open Letter to My Unborn	51
Chapter 9	Lifelong Blessings	65

TABLE OF CONTENTS

Chapter 10	We're All in This Together	73
5150		76
Conclusion		79
About the Author		85

Acknowledgements

God

Sorry we never have had a close relationship verbally. I know I have kept myself distant from you for many reasons, but we both know the issues we have. Even when I had doubt about certain things, you always tried to give me signs that things would end up the way I wanted, but I still had doubt. Once upon a time, I used to believe everything happened for a reason. I was so positive about "the universal laws" and how the world worked, but my dreams were robbed from me. Tainted. My eyes were opened and the realities of this evil world became apparent. I lost trust in you, but you have still blessed me with the desires of my heart. For that, I am grateful.

Physique and Symphinique

I love you both so much. You are my angels from above, sent here just for me. You came out of my belly, and I fell in love. You bring me such joy. The life I once knew is nothing but a distant memory. Every good or bad in my life has led up to you guys being my babies and I wouldn't change that for anything. You were meant for me and I was meant for you. You are a part of me and I am a part of you. We're three Pisces in a pod. Remember that. We shared the same body for 36 weeks and 4 days, so our bond is deep, meaningful and full of love. Never forget how much I love you and will always love you. You were the best part of me. Mama loves you.

Mom

I know I have put you through hell and back and am truly sorry for all the pain and suffering I caused being your daughter. I know it was difficult for you and that there were plenty of times you wanted to give up on me, but you never did. The definition of a mother's love is you. I have been selfish, mean, demanding and disrespectful, so I know it's been hard to love me, but you did. You always said, "I may not like you, but I'll always love you." Thank you for all you have done for me then and now. I am grateful. You love the kids and you are a wonderful grandma. Thanks, mom. I love you.

Dad

I'm sorry I never got to know you and I'm sorry for the years you had to endure living with schizophrenia. It must have been very confusing for you, and I'm sorry the only way you felt you could escape was to end your own life, but where you left off, I picked it right back up. I made it through the maze that you were unable to. So now I will use my voice and experience to help other people fighting mental illness. You are not weak for committing suicide. I see you as strong and can't wait to meet you again so we can catch up.

Pop

You have been one of the most influential people in my life, teaching me so much. Your guidance and what you instilled in me has made me the person I am today. I miss our talks and know if you were here you would have helped me though all the confusion I was going through. I love you and I know we'll meet again; I can't wait. I love you.

Grandma

You mean so much to me. You're the best grandma ever, so the thought of you not being here one day hurts me so bad. I miss pop, but I know you will be in heaven with him and that you'll be happy. If you can give me a sign, try to make it one that I'll be certain is from you. Thank you for loving me unconditionally like you have and for always being here for me. I know it wasn't easy, but you never gave up on me. I love you.

Grandma Vi

You are probably the most spiritual and religious person from both sides of my family. I believe we have that in common among some other things. I know we weren't in each other's lives that much, but we always kept in contact over the phone. I always liked our conversations and the talks we would have. I love you, Grandma. See ya!

RoTanya

You have taught me so much—not only as a woman, but as an individual. You have always been here for me and have never turned your back on me, and I love you for that. If it wasn't for the love we felt at one time, we wouldn't have Physique and Symphinique. Our love created these babies, and I would never want another life. I hope you understand how much you have changed and influenced my whole life. We fuss and fight, disagree and debate, and there is always a battle of the wills between us, but we also depend on each other, need each other, and love each other. I have always been able to confide in you more than anyone else because you understand me mentally and spiritually. We have had deep and meaningful conversations, as well as dreams, hopes, goals and plans. We have built a good life together, including a loving home for our children and a promising future for our grandchildren and the generations after.

I love you. 920+225=228

My family members

I love you all. Thanks for always being there for me and accepting me through the years. It may not have been easy, especially when I was a teenager, but you never gave up on me, so thank you.

My second family (RoTanya's family)

You guys are truly my family, accepting me right away and making me feel like a part of your family. I love you all and I am so glad you guys are in my life.

Tieshena

Thank you for everything, girl. The first time we talked on the phone, we clicked right away. We had the same vision for this book from the beginning. You are not only my publisher, but you've become my mentor and a close friend, and I am so grateful to have met you. I love you and I know I have a friend for life.

People I've wronged

To all the people I've wronged or treated badly over the years, I apologize—unless, of course, you really deserved it.

Introduction

To all family members, friends, acquaintances, coworkers, neighbors, and everyone who knows someone with schizophrenia, I know it's probably difficult to understand or even deal with someone who has a mental illness, but if you take the time to listen to what they are saying, not only will you find it interesting, but you will find truth in what is being said. Don't just dismiss them.

I see people all the time on the street, and it's obvious they are schizophrenic because they're talking to themselves out loud, having a full-fledged conversation. To be normal with a sound mind becomes a distant memory to a schizophrenic. Stuck in between two worlds is our reality. But don't give up on your loved ones. There is light at the end of the tunnel.

Remember, they need you more than you know. Living in a realm that is invisible to you is all they have come to know. Having an understanding and consistent support team is what will help them snap back to reality.

To everyone, including those with schizophrenia, learning a way to understand this illness is critical. Investigate and do your research. A normal and functioning life is possible through medication because it helps balance your brain chemistry by lowering the volume of the voices. The symptoms, however, will always be there. Be the one in control. Don't let Satan control you.

• • •

> *"God will judge us for everything we do, including every secret thing whether good or bad."* – Ecclesiastes 12:14

Ashley DeArkland-Hester

The Invisible Journey

The Kiss of the Devil

Evil is around.

Can you feel it?

He says, "Dance with me."

That means he wants to tango.

Let the games begin.

Even my dreams are corrupted and taunted

By his lies and deception.

All to confuse me.

But I found myself through the maze—

His traps.

He tries to blind me from the truth.

But what is the truth?

It's kinda hard to imagine a world better than this.

So sad if there wasn't.

My glass is half full.

Regardless of my circumstances,

The Invisible Journey

I still keep my head held high.

High as the sky.

However, my mind is dark, deep and full of wisdom.

My heart is bright as the sun.

We all have doubts about things we go through in our lives.

I have learned to calm down because everything will all work itself out!

What do you think happens after we die?

If there is a devil, there has to be a God.

Sound backwards,

But when you personally have a relationship with the devil,

It's difficult to form a bond with God.

These are my feelings through my experiences.

• • •

Journey with me through the mind of a schizo, and I'll show you how far this mind of mine can go...

1

Walk With Me ...

I want to have a relationship with God. I don't always wanna write dark stuff or about the devil. It's so very complicated, but I will try to explain the best I can. People have a voice in their head, but it's their voice. I not only have my own voice in my head, I have a third party in my mind that tries to dictate my every thought. And that party would be the devil himself.

First off, if you have no understanding about schizophrenia, then this may be difficult for you to understand. However, if you are spiritually inclined, then I believe that this is possible. I'm only expressing my personal experiences and how I've rationalized this all. It's madness, dark and so far-fetched. I've talked to plenty of schizophrenics, some fully out of it with no grasp of reality, and they've all mentioned how they get secret messages through music and TV. Understand that every schizophrenic was "normal" or "sane" at one point, then one day they started hearing and seeing things that no one else could.

My first psychotic experience came at the age of 21. Going from being mentally "normal" to clinically insane is very surreal and strange. Is it a curse or a blessing? Instead of looking at mentally ill patients as crazy, look at it as a gift—someone sent with a message. Open your mind and think about it. "Who are they talking to?" Why do we all feel we get negative messages from the radio and TV? Some people aren't as fortunate as others. I'm talking from the perspective of the mentally ill. Families oftentimes don't understand; sometimes they don't even care. They feel burdened and even ashamed to say that they have someone with schizophrenia in their family. So schizophrenics hide it—scared of what society thinks. So what I, Ashley DeArkland-Hester, am proud to say is that:

1) I'm human.

2) I see, hear and feel things that others may not.

3) I am schizophrenic.

4) I am not ashamed of who I am.

Since I started writing a journal at the age of 13 or 14 years old, I always thought about one day trying to make it a book. I mentioned my thoughts about wanting to publish my book to my wife, and she really pushed me to turn my journal entries to a book. Initially, I was hesitant. I knew that I'd be misunderstood and I wasn't ready for all that. Why expose myself and air my dirty laundry? And don't you have to have a degree in psychology to write about mental illness or be a pastor to write about spiritual warfare? *How do I even organize my journal entries?* I wondered. Some entries had dates. Others didn't. Many of them were written without a date on purpose, so I just wasn't sure on how to go about organizing it. The thought of writing a book began to seem overwhelming. At the time, I honestly couldn't even handle success. Or so I thought.

Then I began questioning what my purpose was. Why not share my experiences? I had to think about it. What am I saying that's so wrong? Thousands of people have written books. There are even books out there on the minds of serial killers. So what makes this so different? I'm just talking about the devil and spiritual warfare. I dismissed doubt and decided to go for it because I know that my story will help people understand not only mental illness better, but how it intertwines with spiritual warfare from a schizophrenic woman's opinions and perceptions. If you're open minded and are curious of the unknown, then you will find this to be an interesting read. Well, I hope so at least.

To understand completely where my mind was, is, and hopes to be, get lost with me. Journey with me into the realm of the unknown. Ask yourself, "What would I do? What would I have done to try to save my sanity?"

This game is real. Positions are being played and traps are being set. It's a life full of infiltration, deception, corruption, lies, and confusion. Your objective is to find your way out of the maze.

11:43 PM
5-2-11

Sometimes I feel as though I am possesed. Considering what I experience & what I written already.

It's trippy & 2 be honest I'm still a happy person. I happy w/ my life & the future plans I've made.

I know most of my entries have talked about my experiences, But really they've talked about how my mind works & what I deal w/ on a daily.

2

Everyday is a Battle

There was a time in my life when I went to church every Sunday, but it wasn't until I saw *Passion of the Christ* that I found Jesus. I got saved and baptized for the first time, and that's when my eyes opened and I was introduced to the devil. I was able to hear him so clearly. Yeah, he did trick me because I was very blind to what he was doing and who he really was, and it wasn't until much later that I figured out what I was truly dealing with. It's been so many years now that I've been dealing with him.

Before I got saved and baptized, I had a sane mind. It's like, as my head came out of the water, all hell broke loose. The voices, delusions and hallucinations started. The thoughts he put in my head are so disturbing, but I know wrong from right. I know what's okay and what's not okay. And most of all, I know me. It's saddening to see schizophrenics on the street, or in mental hospitals, so far gone from reality (which you might be thinking that about me) that they can't distinguish between the two. Those individuals can't rationalize what's really going on in their brain. When people think "schizophrenic," they automatically think crazy, psychotic types of people, but if you listen to what they really have to say, a lot of it makes sense. Like me, they receive secret messages from the radio and TV. All the schizophrenics I've talked to have all said the messages are negative, telling them to harm themselves or others. I have the same experiences.

• • •

When I was first diagnosed at the age of 21 years—up until 2006—I had been hospitalized over 19 times. Confused and tricked by the devil. That's why I say that I have a personal relationship with him because we've known each other now for 12 years, which is something I'm not proud of. See, those *whole* 12 years, I had no idea it was the devil attacking me. Like many mentally ill individuals, I tried rationalizing the third party in my head. Can you imagine going through your entire childhood and teenage years, and finally discovering that you are mentally insane at the age of 21?

Let's get something clear. Whether male or female, regardless of your race and economic status, you don't develop symptoms as a child. It kicks in anywhere between ages 16-50. The only real difference is that men usually get their first sign at a younger age than women do. Nonetheless, the first episode is a major shock to your system. Your sane mind knows that something is wrong, so you try to analyze the situation, but you're too confused about what's going on. It's like fighting within yourself to stay alive in a sense. This everyday struggle is a nightmare, and when I say *nightmare*, that's what I mean. My moods go up and down because I'm fighting Satan every single day. Fighting in my mind and keeping my brain strong for this never ending battle. A war between two worlds. An invisible ambush from the pits of hell.

Why is this happening? What is the purpose of an individual being mentally tormented by something so real? Let me, before I finish that thought, explain some things about the devil. He's a liar and a trickster. He twists the truth and blinds you from the light. Please understand I *hate* him. We are enemies. He torments me on a daily, and his ultimate goal is my destruction and downfall. Any joy or happiness I may feel, he tries to steal. Trying to inflict sorrow and sadness instead. He's an intruder in my mind—like a wiretap. That's the gist of my situation, and I write this in hopes of not only helping myself, but helping a lost soul with no direction.

All I have is personal experience, sometimes unaware and blinded from the light. My sixth sense is keen to that of the beast who roams this earth. I'm blessed with the ability to hear, see, feel and think further and deeper than most.

777 = God -vs- 666 = Devil

Spiritual Warfare

terms
- My opinions
  God/Devil
- God (see it's hard to write characteristics for God. Because I really don't ~~recognize~~ know him.)
  - positive
  - helpful
  - parent figure
  - nice
  - quick to anger
  - wants to see you @ ur best
  - pull strings
  - just wanted to talk to him

  - negative
  - attacks/suffering
  - tests (for humans)
  - (confussion)

- Devil
  - Lier
  - Trickster
  - Master of Disguse
  - ~~personal~~ Killer
  - Mass Murder (er)
  - Wanna Bee (Ca)
  - Multipule personalities
  - evil dictator
  - confussion
  - smoke & mirrors

He's Watching Me

So your eyes are open and what do you see?

It seems to be a mystery!

Screaming to God,

But can He hear me searching for positivity?

Looking down on this bottomless pit.

A prisoner of my mind.

He claims he's gonna do something,

But never does.

All he does is pump fear into me

Over certain things I may worry about.

Playing the devil's advocate—

His favorite role.

Waiting to trick me.

Watching me.

Not watching over me to protect me,

But to harm me.

3

Exposing My Reality

When I expose my mental state to people closest to me, I have to feel that they understand what I am telling them. If I feel that they aren't fully grasping what I am telling them, then I'll change the conversation. I expose what I want to. You only know how much I let you know. The one person I feel truly understands and comprehends to the fullest is my wife, RoTanya. She is so spiritually inclined that I trust her enough to expose things to her that I would choose not to share with others.

RoTanya took her time to investigate schizophrenia: the symptoms, the types and all she could research about mental illness. She understands what I am going through psychologically and spiritually. She finds what I'm going through not only super interesting, but "super reality" as well. On top of being schizophrenic, I am also bipolar. So the makings of my mind are as follows: Schizophrenia causes me to hear voices, experience hallucinations and delusions. I get secret messages from the TV and radio, allowing me to communicate with those no one else can see or hear. Other symptoms are confusion, altered perception, and spiritual warfare. Being bipolar causes me to be manic at times. I have mood swings that cause ups and downs, highs and lows. I feel like I'm on cloud nine sometimes and other times I feel as low as the ocean goes. It's like I'm in a mental prison.

That which I described was just the surface of my mind and an idea of how it works. I try to make some sense of all this. I sometimes make up scenarios in my mind and work myself up to the point of going way into left field, but when I'm aware I'm doing it, I stop myself. "Calm down, Ashley," I say. Then I try to bring myself back down into reality. Sometimes I feel I have a brain of an elephant. They never forget and neither do I. From the smallest detail to very important things, especially birthdays, signs and how it all ties into my life.

Certain numbers have certain meanings, and new numbers become meaningful. Sometimes I look at the time on purpose, sign after sign. When I drive, I look at license plates and addresses. I'll be thinking something, and then I'll see a sign that gives me a message. I also retrieve messages from dates, birthdays, death days, marriage dates, barcodes, TV and radio channels, and much more. Basically anything with a number or a sequence of numbers, I will dissect and get the codes I see.

Example: I'm going to look at the barcode on the closest thing near me. I don't know the numbers, but I will get a message out of it either now or in the near future. Sometimes I'll also pick up on patterns. For instance, around October of 2005, I remember watching videos all day long. The videos started serenading me and playing certain songs at certain times like at 2:34. I always saw the number 34. It started at age 13. I would just turn to look at the clock and it was always 34 at least 3-4 times a day. I always looked exactly at ___:34. That's when something was trying to communicate to me. I thought it was my dad, but later on this helped me slow my roll at times. When I saw 34 on clocks, it was like a sign that the entity was saying hi. I'd go into someone's car and it would be 11:34. Or it would pop up in unexpected places such as other's people's clocks, my alarm, car clock, etc. Please believe this is a game. A very dangerous spiritual war. It's all about codes. This is communication in code: demons and angels, good and evil, and peace and torment.

The Meaning of the Numbers!

Ceartin numbers, days, dates, birthday's Death days, Marrayge Dates, Starting & Ending days, Lisence plates, Addressess, bar codes, + v channels, Radio Channels & Much more.

Basically anything w/ a number or a sequence of numbers I will disect & get the codes I see.

O.K example I'm going to look @ this Barcode on the closes thing near me. So I dont know the numbers But, I WILL get a message outta of it. That I will get right then, later, 2morrow or in the near future

I've cut it off the paper box & I will type & disect on the next page.

TIME 7:20 PM
Date 9-18-2011

When a "large
sequence of #"
I see if any 2 or 3
in a row mean
anything to me

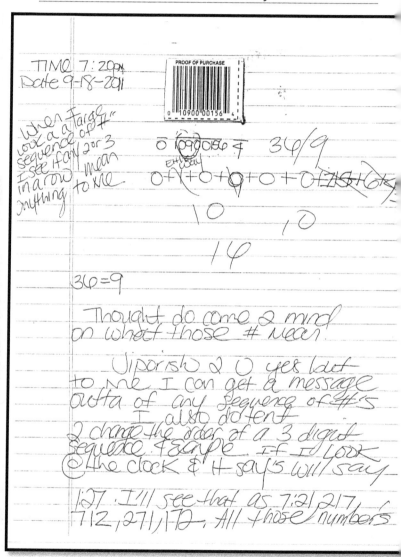

0 1090086 ‡   36/9
        Even
0 + 1 + 0 + 0 + 0 + 0 + 8 + 6 + 0 ✗
                                  10
                                    ,0
                                 10

3+6=9

Thought do come 2 mind
on what those # mean

Viporish 2 U yes but
to me I can get a message
outta of any sequence of #'s
       I also don't
2 change the order of a 3 digit
sequence. Exanple IF I LOOK
@ the clock & it says will say
1:27. I'll see that as 7:21, 217,
712, 271, 172. All those numbers

I see by seeing 1:27 on the clock. (Digital)
When I listen to music I first look @ the length of the song (mins & sec). Then if I'm up to it, I'll write it all down. But, instead I do it all in my head.

Say I'm listening 2 a song & it's @ 34 seconds. Since 34 is a significant # 2 me, I'd listen to what was being said.

So when you see me adding & subtracting #'s on paper. Well, now know you know why!!

Set Up

I'm in a dice game.

I would say for my soul, but I think it's bigger than that.

I say that because there's no question in my mind who my soul belongs to;

And it's not the devil.

Yeah, I ask why…

Because sometimes I get so fed up, but really I too much don't care.

I do know that I'm in a maze.

And I feel set up—

No way out the end of the road, or so am I to believe.

It's hard to believe something better than we all know.

Paradise seems so far-fetched, but would be nice.

Is it possible to be alone in my own thoughts?

Momentarily, perhaps…

But not for long at all.

4

Confrontation

I try so hard to appear as normal as I can. On the outside, at least. I stay well groomed, well-mannered, and I am well-spoken on the outside. Though I'm all put together, sometimes my brain plays tricks on me by making me worry, have anxiety, and fear things I can't control. It's like when you see or read about an angel on one shoulder telling the person why they should or shouldn't do something, and on the other shoulder you got the devil tempting you and making what you want something so appealing. What do you do?

Everyone talks to the voice in their head—their voice of reason, conscious, intuition, etc. They're their best critics and biggest fans. In my case, it's not just me; I have an evil dictator in my mind, invading my personal space. I just happened to talk to my own voice and a third-party evil dictator. I mean really, who do you think schizophrenics are talking to?

Let me guess: You probably didn't care to ever take the time to think about or ponder that question. I'm not a doctor, but I am a clinically diagnosed schizophrenic. I am fortunate to function in society. I take psych meds daily, and some twice a day. I am not ashamed of taking and needing medication. They balance me out!

I fought taking meds for a long time. Some schizophrenics just don't care. They'd rather talk out loud to themselves and be in a full-fledged conversation with whoever they may believe it to be. They've truly lost the grasp on reality, and that's just sad. I am so grateful to have such a supportive family, my wife, and my true friends who all understand me. I am who I am, and I'm proud to be me! I am not ashamed of my lifestyle. If you have a problem with it, then *sorry for ya*. Either you're a believer or you're not. I know I'm not dealing with a demon or multiple demons. The devil himself is who I deal with. He's consistent with his games, voices and tricks. His behavior is too consistent. I know him so very well. A clinical psychiatrist would say that's not reality. *Of course!* They have to say that. And that's what they truly believe. Sorry to inform you, but doctors can be wrong too. It is reality to those who hear, feel, see, and talk to entities that they can't identify.

Know that they are communicating with someone, and I am no exception to the rule. After being diagnosed, it took me seven years before I came to the conclusion who and what I was dealing with. I don't believe in aliens from other planets, so I can say for certain (in my case, at least) that I know it's the devil. He plans his demise for me and my downfall. Like I said, I had a sane mind once upon a time. Yeah, I always overanalyzed things and allowed thoughts to consume me. I was moody, stand-offish, and isolated, but never did I imagine what was in store for my mental state.

Regardless, I am happy and content at this point in my life. Having a third party who invited themselves has become the norm. There's nothing he can say or do that could shock me. I heard, seen, felt everything he's ever felt or thrown on me. I've experienced tragedy at a very young age, and I think all people experience some form of unexpected tragic or horrific event of some type in their lives. If these experiences happened at a young age, then growing up is more difficult emotionally and mentally.

Scattered Thoughts

I grew up not knowing Jesus. Yeah, people try to preach to you. They want to save your soul and whatnot, but at this time in my life, I still am into astrology and numerology. When I first meet a person, I ask them their sign because it better helps me understand the person.

I understand that religious people believe those spiritual interpretations are the devil's playground. As mentioned before, my religious beliefs are somewhat unorthodox. That's in no way to say that I'm an unbeliever, however. If there's a devil, then there has to be a God. A blessing in disguise. For instance, I don't know why, but sometimes I feel God's hand is on my brain when I write.

When I feel I'm having a moment, a positive interaction with the good side, then the devil steps in and the angels and God back up, which makes me feel upset. Like, why would God be allowing all this to happen? And why can't you question God? In my case, am I supposed to just accept the things that I've been exposed to? Many religious people feel that questioning God is off limits, but I don't necessarily agree with that. I try to be the best person I can be. I try to be honest and forthright, and God does know my heart. I had a false image of God and His personality. I always blamed him for everything I was going through, questioning who was really in control—God or Satan. Why was the world suffering and why so many horrible things—oppression, discriminations, wars, etc.—happening to human beings. So since that, I have realized that we're more alike than I thought. I see and understand God as a friend instead of an enemy. He knows the issues we have, and that's what He and I need to work on.

My trust has been broken, so now I have a wall up. I can hear Him and I know the signs of Him reaching out, but I don't reach back. The reason I feel this way is for me and the world. You got people starving, no clean water, and hunger all over the world. People don't think about that as they live their daily lives, and it breaks my heart. When you open your eyes and realize what is going on in the world today, it's pure chaos. Yeah, I do believe He watches over the good people, but we're suffering too.

> *"The whole world is under the control of the evil one"*
> *– 1 John 5:19*

• • •

As I'm writing this right now, the song that I'm listening to just said "sell your soul." That's one way that the devil communicates with me. I'll have a thought and the song answers the question. Or the song might say a word that I was just in the middle of saying, writing, or thinking. This is how the communication between me and the spirits go. They have no voice, so in order to communicate, it has to be a way for me to receive it.

It's like a game of Charades. The first word leads you to an object which sparks a thought that leads you to your next clue, second word, and so on. So what's your objective? Think about it. Where did that thought take you? Pay attention to how your mind works, your thought process. Be aware and open-minded, and you might figure it out.

The Beast controls Everything from the Paver to markus people. By being marked you ~~took~~ signed your soul to the Devil. You got marked on your right hand. If you didn't have a mark on your right head

You could not buy food. Work or anything. So I assume they were left the starve. I think but am not sure but I believe if you weren't more a You believes in your Jesus Christ was to strong God would

6

Discovery & Confirmation

I spoke to my mom recently, and she said I started having symptoms at the age of nine. That surprised me. She said I had a bad temper and mood swings. I didn't think my anger issues kicked in until my teenage years. I do remember in elementary school having to go to a teacher's house to see her husband who was a therapist. Oh, I hated going. It's kind of sad for me to hear this—to have had issues so young; it's heartbreaking. I couldn't even imagine my children going through what I went through at such a young age. I also remember, after my dad died, my mom putting me in a study for children who underwent traumatic experiences.

My father committed suicide on August 15, 1985 from a self-inflicted stab wound to the chest. He was also schizophrenic. I don't know much about my father, only what my family members have told me. I have asked questions, and I've tried to form my own idea of who my father is and was. My mom told me that he didn't want me to see him in that state. She mentioned that when he was diagnosed, they basically told him he'll live his days in an institution. At that point they didn't have too many psych meds. Plus, he didn't like taking meds and didn't want to live his life like that.

I shouldn't have any type of ill will towards him, which I don't. I can't blame him for his mental state, but I do think maybe that's where a lot of my anger comes from. It used to bother me about my father, but one day I just got numb to the pain that I was feeling. My family tells me he loved me and that he wanted them to make sure I knew he loved me. I do feel that he does try to reach out to me. All these years I have always ignored it, but since I've had my kids, it has softened my heart a little. My son, Physique looks just like my dad. It's a trip. I don't know how it would be if I had a dad. When I think about it, it's kind of weird.

We are human and make mistakes. Yes, I mentioned I don't have a relationship with God, but I have my opinions and beliefs. For starters, whenever I do attempt to heal my relationship with God, the devil gets louder and I end up more confused. To avoid all of that, I'd just rather maintain my distance. I do know the Bible says that a person either bares good or bad fruit, and that "You must go through [Jesus] to get to the Father." Well, when I do pray, I pray to God, Himself. I do believe in Jesus, but I go directly to the man. I do things my way when it comes to how my relationship is. It's complicated, but it's me and God's relationship. I have my reasons.

He allowed Satan to make me believe so many horrible things are true. One of them being that all people are bad. God knows what each person has done in their past and has the power to throw me, along with all the righteous people, in hell and torture us.

There is no excuse for what He allows to go on. For instance, He allows Satan to continue to have all his power and over the centuries it has corrupted you. It has turned your once pure heart evil and wicked. How could you all have allowed that to happen? You should have been stronger than this. Why did God make a wager with the devil to see if Job would turn to God if God took all he had? If by taking all his stuff, would it shake Job's faith, and who would he turn to? Why test a man who you already knew was not going to go to the devil?

I just finished this book with great points on this subject. Now some of the author's opinions I disagree with, but for the most part I related to the book, which is about God. Basically I took it as more of a personal opinion of the writer—how he feels about God and religion. I am not an avid reader, but saw this man on the morning news show I watch. I found his arguments to be interesting and the book appealed to me. He questions God's existence and asks why, if God is all good and all-knowing, he allows so much pain in people's lives. He also talks about heaven, hell, death, etc. He not only gives his opinion, but states facts from the Bible and facts from history of the human race. He makes it clear that he's agnostic, which I didn't know what that meant. I looked it up and learned that agnostics (in my own words and interpretation) take the position of that they don't know if God exists, whereas atheists believe there is no god.

It was an informative book and a good read because, as you've noticed, I also question God. I, too, believe a lot of what this book talks about. Do I now believe I'm agnostic? No, I'm not. I know there is a devil because I deal with his torture and torment on a daily. Therefore, there has to be a God. To some that may sound backwards, and most people probably would have phrased that differently saying they know there is a God, and therefore there must be a devil. But I feel I don't know God. Doesn't mean I don't believe in Him; I just have so many questions.

Supposedly writing down how your thinking is supposed 2 paint a picture for the reader. I'd rather have a verbal conversation. I wonder if I paint the picture of the real me, were people get the right picture & not getting it twisted. I feel if someone were 2 read my thoughts & feelings without actually knowing me, seeing me & my demenor. People will always think the way they think the way they preceive.

7

My Intuition is Key

I feel most people kiss ass to go to heaven and praise God without questioning Him. When I do talk to God, I talk to Him as an equal, which is another statement people might feel is backward thinking. *God's not your equal.* He's your superior, right? He's almighty, but I'm sorry for myself. I'm not going to start our conversation. Lord, Father God, etc. Enough about that. When all you hear in your own mind is noise and confusion, how do you praise God when the devil is all in your face? Most people would say that's when you should praise Him the most, saying "I rebuke you" or "No weapon formed against me shall prosper."

It's so sad to say I know the devil personally, and he laughs at statements like that. Who do you believe in? God or the devil? Evil or good? I choose God and good. However, I have a lot of questions, fears, beliefs, etc. that I need and want answered. Once upon a time, I thought for myself. The only voice in my head was mine. Shit, not anymore. It's like I'm chained, handcuffed to the devil. But who has the key? Who's really in control? And if God created us all, why does it matter who I choose to love?

I have an attitude of *if loving you is wrong, I don't wanna be right*. Some people feel that two women together is wrong. More Christians/conservatives feel that way, but in my eyes they're wrong. I never thought I'd love a woman, but it happened and I'm the happiest I've ever been. My life is filled with joy. So are you telling me that God is not happy for me or He's up in the sky, looking down, preferring me to be miserable? I thought that was the devil's job!

I don't know about you, but I'm not gonna deny my heart. Yeah, supposedly we're in the flesh and we're only feeding into worldly desires, but I don't love RoTanya with my flesh. I love her with my soul. And supposedly when we die, our soul is what either goes to hell or heaven.

So what then? Just because my environment changes, my feelings are supposed to change? How can anybody tell you who you can love? That makes me wonder what heaven is. A communist country? Even though it's not a country, most communist countries are ruled by one ruler, and, in this case, that ruler would be God. It's like back in the day when countries were ruled by a king and queen. Yeah! We don't know what that feels like to be under rulers like that, but if you really sit and think about how heaven might be and try to analyze it, then that's some of the things I'd think of.

I imagine people up there worshipping all day long. Hallelujah, all day? I mean think about it. God's supposed to be the person who loves and understand you the most. He wants you to come to Him. He wants to be your friend, and He gave you free will, right? Well, I'm going to follow my heart and not worry about my salvation. My heart and soul comes first and is important to me. My intuition is key! Yes, I love a woman. I'm married and no one is gonna make me feel ashamed or have regrets or doubts. And we're going to have a baby! Well I'm going to carry the baby, but the baby is hers just like she carried in her stomach. We also planned for the child to carry her last name so we would always have a connection to each other—just as if we were a man and a woman who had a baby.

We will be connected for eternity. Supposedly, time doesn't exist in heaven. It's infinite. My love works the same way. It's never ending. This is how I feel deep inside. My mind, body and soul feels this way, and no one can change that. It's spiritual warfare.

205 = Courage
920 = when I was publized in this case, not meaning my wife's B-Day

[205] [1920]
TEST

10:10 Time

1010 = Me
1010 = Engaged

6 [1920] 8
FAITH

920 again's - Ro Jenya's B-Day & my 3rd time Dude publized

23 [825]
WHY

825 = The original Dude we were supposed 2 get married

Not askering my question going into it's own direction

12 9115 = 911 Ambulance
LIKE 115 - saved from Death

TR
2015
SEE
1955

PEOPLE 515 7 Pnsion
105151025   5167
                    #920
struggle   177 - No we from God
1920 4 177 125

Tallan But what when I was found in the hallway of my apt in front of Apt #115 find By neighbor who called 911 cus I was unconscious laying in the hallway

Dive Deep

Not knowing me personally,

You might get the wrong impression of me.

A look into someone's mind can be interesting and exciting at first—

But the deeper you go the darker it will get.

Do you think you can handle diving deep into your own psyche?

Analyze, look ahead, plan and be wise.

I was forced to dive deep, deep inside of myself.

I've overanalyzed and have gotten consumed with situations and maybe an experience.

Amputate Satan's last leg for stand.

He's losing his mind, but he wants more.

He's trying to talk to me, so of course me being who I am, I must respond.

This ain't living;

We need help.

Don't think you're untouchable with superpowers or a supreme being.

You claim this is your world and you're the ruler, but sorry to break it to you that you're not.

Can you understand me or does what I say seem like riddles to you?

Could it be a third eye or a sixth sense?

ESP, Telepathy and telekinesis or all the above?

If you had the choice of any superpower you could possess, what would it be?

Would you use it for evil or for good?

Without preaching, we all know right from wrong—

Or we should.

And if you don't care either way, well sorry for ya!

I have some idea's that have come to me. If you can't tell by now I sometime think far into the future. Try to predict whats going to happen. I jump the gun & conclusions. But I'm not perfect. As I decide to think @ things from a spiritual point of view. I fully understand I am human & I'll never be perfect.

Open Letter to My Unborn

2/19/04

To my children,

Word of life, love and wisdom to my children. The family you came from and the history of generations before you. I'm writing this so you have an understanding of my life before you guys were born. That's why it's important to me that you are open and express yourselves. I'll never know your personalities until I have you all. I hope you see that what I do for you all is to push you as people. I'll push you to be your best and challenge your minds anyway possible. If any of you should fall, I'll pick you up. If any of you happen to wander off your path. I will guide you back in the right direction.

Know all that I do is for love. Sometimes I might seem hard, but it is for your own good. I will always explain things to you while I'm doing this. I'll be showing you through my actions the right way.

Since this is being written before I have my family, who knows how our family will be, but I do know that I will raise you to be a close-knit family. My goal will be to keep all of my kids close and safe. Please always stick together. Depend on each other. Growing up, I was an only child. Cherish your brothers and sisters. At least you all have each other. I had to depend on myself and teach myself survival skills. I plan to celebrate every holiday—from Hanukkah to Christmas, Thanksgiving, Passover, Easter, 4th of July, birthdays, Halloween and Kwanza. All Jewish, Christian, Catholic, and Muslim holidays too because I want you all to learn the diversity of the world.

Be proud of your Jewish and African descent. You know throughout history, both cultures have been made to feel subhuman. Since biblical times, Jews were slaves. In the 1940s, Hitler, who felt that Jews were less than human, ran Germany and most of Europe. His army marched through the streets with their guns, pushing Jews to stay in line. All Jews had to move out of their homes, give all their jewelry, antiques, clothes, furniture and all possessions to the Germans. They were then sent to camps where they were gassed or shot in the streets. Killing over 6 million (not sure exactly how many he killed), but Hitler slaughtered the Jews with no remorse.

In the 1600s through 1950s and 60s, Blacks were also made to feel less than human. In the 1600s, the White man went over to Africa and ambushed, forcing Africans to board ships and come to the US. They were then sold like cattle to slave traders to work on their plantations. Moms and kids were sold separately. Families were torn apart. African Americans were beat, and even the women were raped by the slave owners. Thanks to Abraham Lincoln and the Civil War, slaves were set free in 1865.

However, the problems still arose, holding back Blacks. They didn't want Blacks to join the army, vote, get schooling or anything to better themselves. In the 1950s and 60s, in the South, Blacks were harassed and the KKK was at work. The KKK is a White supremacy group, who would burn crosses in front of Black homes and churches. The 50s and 60s was the civil rights movement with Dr. Martin Luther King as the leader. He held boycotts, rallies, and speeches to protest the injustice. He won the Nobel Peace prize and was eventually murdered because he was trying to promote peace. The White man couldn't stand it.

Both Jews and Blacks have felt the disrespect and the underserved hatred from the fellow race. People have looked at Jews and Blacks as though they were wild animals who should be controlled and locked in a box, separated from the rest of society. I think that's why I wanted to have biracial children. Superhuman. Jesus was a Jew. I wanted to have kids who were Black Jews. (In the Jewish religion, the child is whatever their mom is). Jews and Blacks are blessings from God, and God favors those who are wrongly done. The devil always does his job, stirring up chaos. People who don't have to face race really can't understand that race is a major factor in the game called life.

Times have gotten better, but a person's race is still a place of how they are viewed. All the stereotypes stick with that race and people start to believe them. All I'm saying is be true to yourself. Be proud of your heritage. Value it and pass it down to your kids.

Now a little advice and words of wisdom to carry with you always. Strive to be your best. Never let anyone discourage you and your goals. Always express yourselves and tell people how you feel. If you don't tell a person what's bothering you, they'll never know. If they don't know what's bothering you, they can't change it. Make people aware of what's wrong. Be direct and honest. Don't lie. People can tell when a person's a liar. You'll always be looked at as a liar and no one will take you seriously like the boy who cried wolf. I also want to teach you about God and the afterlife. Spiritually and laws of the universe. His holiness. Whatever you feel most comfortable saying. I started out studying astrology, then reincarnation, spirits, afterlife, psychic abilities, dream interpretation, tarot cards and alchemy.

I feel, to some degree, I am psychic. I'm very intuitive with the supernatural; it actually is quite natural for me. I understand the other side better than I do this side. I'll always keep searching for answers to unlock the mystery of life. Having to depend on myself, I taught myself to tap into my higher consciousness. I've tapped into past life experiences. Numerous times, I've dreamt of things before they happened. I've always dreamed since I was a child. I taught myself that when I'm dreaming, I'm aware that I'm dreaming. It's called lucid dreaming and allows you to control your dreams and asks questions in your dreams. When I was 16, I learned how to meditate. This taps into the transcendental, opening your consciousness.

All in all, I'm trying to push you to your full potential. To be the best that you can be. I know that I can make it, that I can stand, no matter what may come my way. Jesus, my life is in His hands. Ask God and He will show you that He heard your prayers. No matter what happens, God sees all. Everything happened for a reason. Every person you meet, every situation in your whole life is a blueprint. You're following the directions of God's will. Understand you're here to work through certain issues. Certain hurdles and challenges that your soul require.

You kids were meant to be mine. I'm meant to be your mama. We're here to learn certain things from each other. My main issue is my anger, aggression and temper. I must learn how to be tactful and diplomatic. I tend to fly off the handle and not think before I speak. Now I'm only 21 and haven't had you kids yet, but I think at least one of you will teach me how to be more balanced. I also think one of you will be just like me. We might even clash with one another. No matter what, we're teaching each other. As a family, we're going to argue and fight. Promise no matter what we will always stick together. Promise that we'll tell one another how we feel. Even if it might hurt someone's feelings. Helping each other grow as human beings. Telling each other what bothers us, discussing it and then coming to an agreement of the problem and finally moving on once a middle ground is reached. Always talk openly with each other will help us grow as a family. Friends will come and go, but a family is bonded by all the experiences that we share as a whole. Going through things together and winning as a team.

I say this to you, my children. I love you and you're my blessing. Please take my advice as a little window into the person that your mother is. Now I'm going to give a brief description on some people who are close and important to me and my life. My Pop Pop is the second husband of my mother's mom, my Grandma Sandy (just Grandma). Since my mom worked all the time, Pop and Grandma always watched me. Me and Pop were closer than a peanut butter and jelly sandwich. He taught me how to swim, ride my bike, count money, add and subtract, along with many other things.

When I was little, we spent a lot of time at the pool and parks. I used to pretend I was at a restaurant. I was the waitress and Pop would order breakfast. I would make eggs and coffee, charge him, count the money and give him change. We also played games, especially cards like Gin Rummy. He was very involved and was a hands-on grandfather. I mentioned him first because he was the most pivotal, important person in my life. I hold him responsible for molding and pushing me to my fullest potential. He's the one who got me into magnet from 2nd grade to 7th grade. He called everyone he could to get me in and he did. I was a living nightmare, a trouble maker, hard-headed, stubborn and very unpleasant to be around. I was angry at the world. Pop thought I was in trouble. During those years we weren't as close. I didn't talk to him as much as I could've because I was hard to deal with.

I turned around when Pop got into a car accident. He fell asleep while driving and crashed. He was in the hospital for three months. That is when I realized I could lose him. After his accident, we became really close again. This was now an adult relationship. That's when we really started to communicate. I could talk to him about anything. He was always up for a conversation. I knew I could trust him about school and my problems. I told him about the interests I had and the new ventures I wanted to take on. He would just give me advice, tell me stories of his life, and then relate it to what problem I was having. He gave me his wisdom and experiences. He always was interested in what I was doing. Always ready to lend an ear.

He showed me how to really love someone. I felt he understood me, which made me more open. He taught me how to communicate and how to be open and express my feelings. That's why I was telling you guys to always communicate and express your feelings. Pop had a big role in my life. I loved him more than anyone I've known. Pop showed me how to be a better person, how to take a person and treat them with an overwhelming amount of love, affection, care, wisdom and emotional support. No matter what project I wanted to do, he inspired me to see it through. If I ever had a problem, I called Pop. He could just shoot the shit. Take a topic, analyze it, dissect it and talk about it in depth until all angles are covered.

Now that he's gone, all my feelings stay inside. I can't tell my friends how I feel. If I need to yeah, but mostly I counsel myself. That's why I say I'm a loner. I told my mom, "Mom, in five years, I'm afraid nothing's going to change and everything will be the same. Are you afraid of that?" She said, "Yeah, I think about it all the time." That's all she said.

Before I have my kids, I know you guys will be mixed with black. I want you kids to know about both of your heritages. It's important not to forget those before you. A brief description of my dad's side of the family. My dad is the baby of five. Denise, the twins (Dale and Diana), Jim then my dad. I grew up close to my mother's side of the family. My mom's side is very close. Every Hanukah, Passover and Thanksgiving, we all get together—ever since I was little.

I always felt different than my family. They didn't make me feel like an outsider; I just did. I was closest to Pop. I really didn't get to know my family until Pop died. During all the family get togethers, I was with Pop. After Pop died, I felt so alone. Since I was so close to Pop I didn't really get to know Grandma until Pop passed. Since Pop died, Grandma is a social butterfly. She is always out: movies, cards, plays, dinner, and vacations. She's never home, which is why I always try her cell phone first. This is the first time she's been alone in 30-40 years. Her and Pop socialized a lot too, but now she's even more social. She has a dry personality—not to me, but to others maybe. Not rude or standoffish, just a little serious. Then again, she's Russian, and Russians are very serious. I'm pretty serious myself. She's also very generous though. When we were little, my grandparents got us stocks and bonds. She's what keeps the family together. She is loving and sacrifices a lot for her family. I guess she keeps busy so she doesn't think about Pop.

Now my dad's family is different. I figured that out as I got older. They don't get together on Thanksgiving and Christmas. Everyone does their own thing. I don't know my dad's side of the family to well. I have always talked to my Grandma Vi; we have had a pretty close relationship. We always have deep conversations and talk a lot on the phone. It used to bother me that I wasn't close to my dad's side of the family.

That's why it's important that we're close. I've lost one parent and only have my mom and Grandma left (also aunts and uncles), but I'm closest to Mom and Grandma. When I raise you guys, the life I had will only be in memory. I'm scared to get older because losing my family will be so hard.

Cherish the time you have because tomorrow's not promised. Even after I'm gone, please keep the family close. Don't forget who you are and where you came from. Lean on each other for guidance and support.

Love, Laugh, Live Life.

Love,

Your Mama

9

Lifelong Blessings

Me and RoTanya have been together for three years and married for one. Besides my mother, she was the only one who truly understood and accepted me for who I was. During that time, we were also family planning. We were ready to grow our love and start a family of our own. I'd gone to the doctor for a consultation and learned the steps that it would take to become impregnated. That didn't stop the devil though. He made it clear that he could care less if an innocent baby was growing in my belly.

I was once told that I don't need to be a mother. Well, that statement was made by a dummy. I needed and wanted to be a mother. Being a mother would make me feel normal because I knew that I wouldn't be alone. Once my mother and grandmother passed, I didn't want to be alone. I wanted a family. We deserved the opportunity of being a family, of being parents of a healthy baby. Plus, I had two abortions when I was younger and always regretted it.

We were blessed to be able to do in vitro fertilization (IVF), which was an exciting, expensive and terrifying experience. If it didn't happen the first try, then I wasn't sure that we would have enough money to go a second round. So we started the process. I started taking prenatal pills along with dhea pills to help me produce more eggs. I started to take shots to control my ovulation, then I took shots to help me produce more eggs, and after that a patch to thicken my uterus then my eggs were extracted. I had produced 19 eggs, which were watched by an embryologist. Five out of the 19 were good eggs. Five days later, they transferred two.

I was on bed rest for three days after my transfer. The doctor told me that if there was any bleeding, then my chances of being pregnant were slim, so I made sure to follow all the instructions. As I waited for the results, the devil took that chance to mess with me. I would have dreams of bleeding while in the shower. Fortunately, I recognize when things happen at the hands of the devil. Two weeks later, I took a blood test and I was pregnant. Though he planted fear in me throughout my whole pregnancy, I still birthed two beautiful and healthy babies.

I got pregnant the first cycle of IVF, so I do feel blessed. I have three eggs still frozen, and I'd like to get pregnant again soon. I will forever be grateful to their father. I only know this man through his profile, but I know he must be special because he entered my life from a distance, and with God's help, I have two angels from above.

• • •

The things I have learned, realized and experienced recently have opened my mind so much. My view of people, the world and life have all changed. Not my personal belief, but the way I see people, the world and life is in a very clear and realistic light. What I have realized makes me sad. I ask God what I should do. I feel alone. I feel no one understands me. Just my grandfather and he's gone. I miss him. He was a great man. I really came to a realization about my family this past weekend. So much stuff has been going on, it is amazing. I also was concerned about my life, career and my purpose. What am I going to do?

I have some ideas that have come to me. If you can't tell by now, I sometimes think far into the future, trying to predict what's going to happen. I always think about the future and I like to plan things out. I try to foresee how things will turn out, and RoTanya tells me I can't predict the future.

The Invisible Journey

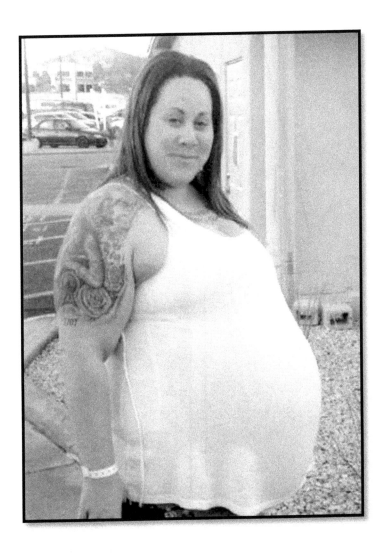

The Invisible Journey

10

We're All in This Together

As I decide to think about things from a spiritual point of view, I freely understand that I am human and I'll never be perfect. All I write and express in my opinion is how I perceive what's going on mentally with me. Other schizophrenics explain what goes on in their brains by the way they're feeling and thinking. They perceive it in their own way, which makes sense to them in their minds. Some of my views have changed for the better, and I see things in a more positive light. As I sit here, I think of my life and what means the most to me. Sometimes I get confused, overwhelmed and my perception is off. I jump the gun and act off emotions.

What is life? We're born to die. We die to live and we live to die. It's so sad. I don't have a degree to back up my opinion. I'm not going to say I have a theory about mental illness or spiritual warfare. All I have is personal experience. Even right now those people are just watching me. I can't see them, but they can see me. They're talking to me as I write. They never are satisfied and continuously test me on every thought I have. It's always been a lot of tormenting from them. Pushing my buttons. They constantly test my character. They would put me in situations, watch me and analyze how I would respond.

Right now, for instance, the voices are saying that I'm showing off and trying to remind them of how I acted before. They wanted to see, through my actions, how my real character would respond in an unexpected situation. My mind and heart have always been pure until those voices came along. See, the mind is a crazy, dark, weird, cold place. And when you're not alone in your own brain, it can be very violent and disturbing for those spies who listen, along with those who try to talk to you. Like I said before, once upon a time, I was a sane individual.

Always aggressive and confrontational, but never allowing myself to get close to anybody. I always kept to myself. A lone wolf. An only child and a loner, but dealt with it. I know there is a positive force watching over me, especially when I get those positive, uplifting codes. It's hard to try and pick up that feed because the devil starts playing tricks like it was him the whole time. I've got to figure this out and why this is happening to me. Why do I live in a nightmare and what the fuck does he really want from me? I don't have any special talent. I don't sing or act. So what does he want from me? Like I tell him all the time, it's not like he's assigned to me. Nobody is holding a gun to his head forcing him to be around me 24/7.

It's like I'm in a constant battle of spiritual warfare against evil forces. In some way, we're all dealing with this battle. We're all born with a curse that stands in the way of you and righteousness. Mine happens to be schizophrenia, having a personal relationship and a direct connection with Satan.

Not many could handle this reality. Not many understand it, but a large part of my purpose in this world is to spread awareness, to remove the stigma and fear that's associated with schizophrenia, and to help others see that mental illness is a different battle within the same spiritual war that they are in. We're all in this together.

5150

You all pray for my downfall.

You would love if I blew my brains out or stab myself like daddy did,

But that won't happen because I'd rather get murdered like a slaughtered pig.

Ripped open from the inside out.

See they played the same game with daddy,

But he layed it down just to prove it.

They may call him a coward,

But to stab yourself in the heart and die slow for 8-10 minutes—

Only a real man could endure.

See 5150s run in this fam;

And this one right here is an animal who switches form when needed.

See I'm a truth teller.

A single person doing this damn thing all alone.

What thing?

We keep this thing silent.

Who are we?

Honey, don't you know what a 5150 is?

If not, you better.

Conclusion

No matter what I have been through in my life, I wouldn't change a thing. It has all led me to where I am now. I'm grateful for the life I am living because at one point, I was headed toward self-destruction. Though I fight everyday within myself, I do have a peace of mind— now that I have my two beautiful twins, my son, Physique and my daughter, Symphinique. I'm still amazed that me and RoTanya finally had the two babies we'd planned.

Having children makes me feel normal. That's what normal people do, have kids. They feed them, bathe them, change them, guide them, learn from them, love them, and get loved back. My son and my daughter are the only ones I can completely let my guard down with: act silly, play, watch TV, run around, and laugh. It's exciting being a mother. Not only has being a mother brought joy, but has taught me a lot. It's let me understand a little more about GOD. I understand that certain things people go through are for their own good sometimes. If I tell my kids no, it's for a good reason. When I say don't touch that because it's dangerous, I'm doing it for their own good to keep them safe. It makes me think of Adam and Eve and how God told them they can eat from any tree except this one particular one. He told them for a reason. He knew the outcome, but just like a kid, if you tell them not to do something, they want to do it more.

I know what God means when He says He wants people to believe in Jesus. That's His son. It's like, if you can't accept my son, then you can't accept me. If someone didn't accept my children...see ya later! *Bye*! I put my children before everyone else. I also believe that God probably wanted a child for Himself. After all, it's the best feeling in the world to be a parent, raising your own flesh and blood.

I may be a lot of things, but a bad mother I am not. No one can ever take that away from me. I live for my children; they are my life. All my life's uphill battles has prepared me to be as strong as I am. Though Satan will always be a right there perpetrating, I'll never let him defeat me. I have fought him all these years and will continue to do so for the rest of my years. Though my relationship with

God is still distant, my heart is slowly softening about everything that I have experienced. As long as God and Satan are at war, we are all at war.

My perception of things have changed drastically. I see things more clearly now. This is bigger than me. There are billions of human beings on earth, and everyone is going through some type of battle. The world we live in today is evil. Satan has a hold of people's minds, and they don't even realize it. The things humans are doing in the world is sick and heartbreaking. Children are getting abused physically and sexually every day, raped at four and five years old, even murdered. People are killing each other, police killing people, human trafficking, animal abuse, wars, innocent bloodshed, starvation, corruption, racism, an unjust criminal system, dictatorship, lies, deceit, malicious acts of hate, jealousy, envy, predators in schools and churches, manipulation, cover ups, disregard for another human's soul or anything living. Knocking down someone else just because, or for your own benefit. Hate, period. These are the issues of the world today. Open your eyes, and protect your kids and yourselves. Things are really serious in this world we live in.

That is why I bless my babies with Holy water every night before they go to bed. I also blessed them every day when I was pregnant. If I don't protect my kids, who will? You can't trust anybody nowadays. It's a sad situation. That's why I feel my heart is softening towards God because of Satan plays for keeps. It's because of Satan that the world we live in is so bad. Everybody is turning on each other and are only out for themselves. God is the only who protects us. Because if it was up to Satan, we would all be dead.

What people fail to realize is that we all die. There's no exception. Even Satan's puppets doing his work here on earth are going to die. Whether poor or rich, fate is all the same. Death is inevitable. All you have done in secret will be exposed. You were and are being watched. Everything you've done has been recorded. When you are sitting there on judgment day and your whole life is on a big screen, showing you that you were not alone and all you have done good or bad, what are you going to say? Everyone will be judged. Life here on earth was a test of character, morals, values, honor, loyalty and respect. You either bare good fruit or bad fruit. Life is too short. Get it together because there is no coming back from death.

About the Author

Never shying away from who she is or what she was called to do, **Ashley DeArkland-Hester** goal is to educate others about schizophrenia and to encourage those with mental illness to live fully and not feel alone in their experiences.

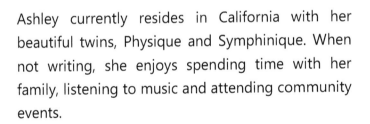

Ashley currently resides in California with her beautiful twins, Physique and Symphinique. When not writing, she enjoys spending time with her family, listening to music and attending community events.

Learn more about Ashley at
www.AshleyDeArklandHester.com

WE WANT TO HEAR FROM YOU!!!

If this book has made a difference in your life Ashley would be delighted to hear about it.

Leave a review on Amazon.com!

BOOK ASHLEY TO SPEAK AT YOUR NEXT EVENT!

Send an email to booking@publishyourgift.com

Learn more about Ashley at
www.AshleyDeArklandHester.com

FOLLOW ASHLEY ON SOCIAL MEDIA

  @WalkWithAshley

 /WalkWithAshley

"EMPOWERING YOU TO IMPACT GENERATIONS"
WWW.PUBLISHYOURGIFT.COM

CPSIA information can be obtained
at www.ICGtesting.com
Printed in the USA
BVHW052315270623
666442BV00015B/859